God is a Woman

T.J. McGowan

ALSO BY TJ MCGOWAN

We Are Not One Thing

Timeless Gardens & Other Beautiful Miseries

God is a Woman

QUERENCIA

Querencia Press, LLC
Chicago Illinois

QUERENCIA PRESS

© Copyright 2022
T.J. McGowan

LIBRARY OF CONGRESS CATALOG-IN-PUBLICATION DATA

ISBN 979 8 9860788 7 8

.

www.querenciapress.com

First Published in 2022

Querencia Press, LLC
Chicago IL

Printed & Bound in the United States of America

I do not pray. I do not believe there is an invisible man watching me sleep and eat and jerk-off. I have no need for organized pursuits of fear to oppress people into following a set of rules. No need for brick buildings and altars, or leather bound books. I am not concerned with the afterlife. We've all already been dead before inception and I can't remember a single thing about it. No Deity kept me company when I couldn't exist. I do not look up to see it in the sky, when it already walks among me on Earth. Instead, I search root and tree. I attend church of flesh and form. I sing hymnals of body and mind, where the cosmos mirrors the womb. This is the closest I can get to an identifiable idea of God. Not one that hides in the folds of where we can't look, but one that lives in the beauty of feminine power right before our eyes. I place my faith like a seed in the soil and water it with the celestial cup of woman - the only God that matters.

-T.J. McGowan

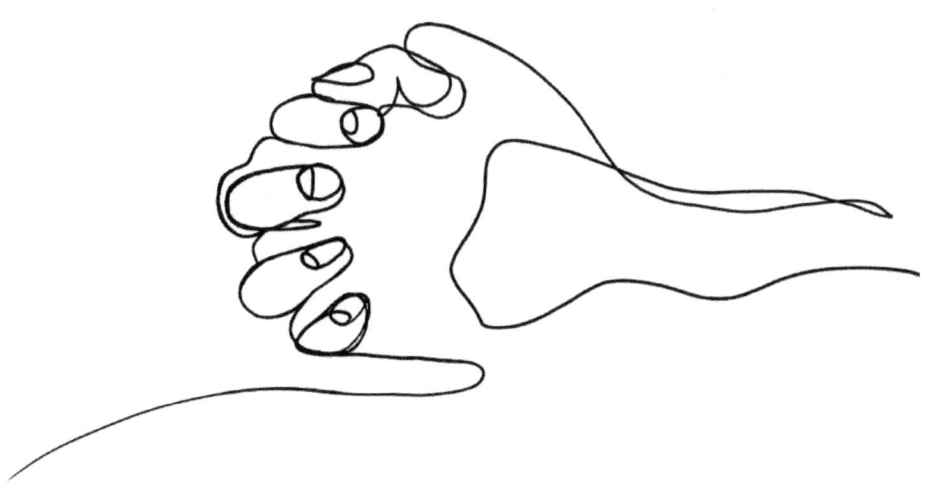

Ache

I am enamored,
Swallowed whole
By your existence,
Adrift in oceans
I beg to drown me.

You pull me closer to belief.
Closer to an idea of truth.

You are trouble and peace.
Answers to unknown
and potion of desire.

I need you in flesh and memory.
And, somewhere in the beyond.

I pen scripture for skin
and pray to the taste of your mouth.

You are chrome and obsidian.
A dark, alluring church,
and I ache to find God
inside you.

Honesty

Honesty inhabits your bones
and falls from your tongue
like summer rain.
Sweet and wet and warm
and deliberate.
Alive unlike others.
Seeing more than we are meant to.
Eye of internal wonder,
birth of new days
In the roots
of perpetual healing.
You are beautiful.
Colossal in quietude.
A fever, always trembling
beneath the surface.
You are blue crystal
and red skies,
momentous and rare

Vessel

A vessel of flesh and beauty,
with light bent at its curves,
you exist in the fluid marriage
of truth and cosmic questions.
Particles crashing into form.
Eyes of glass pulling dreams from the mind.
Lips of secret language searching for words
that perfect the nature of your thoughts.
A body of celestial pose,
summoning all elements into peace.
I fall into the tumble of desire - into the echoes
and dust of a room you once inhabited.
I track the history of the world to find you
and listen to untold stories.
Legends where darkness subsides
and horizons forfeit the sun to your smile.

Melody

Command me to feed
your heart,
throbbing and pumping
sweet melody.
Acoustic fingerprint
echoing into the mystery
of night
and passing life.
Reach in and drag
the fever to my lips,
where I hold no fear of death
in comparison
to kissing you the wrong way.
I want to leave warm flowers
in your mouth,
trail the petals
back to quiet places,
A patch of grass
away from the collapse
of humankind,
where you can pull songs
from my throat
and let them stretch under the sun
for you.

Breathe

I want you like bathwater,
all at once,
and everywhere.
Sweat-stained tongue
and fingertips of molasses.
I feed on you, slowly.
Hold your pulse in my teeth.

Breathe for me.

Tell me with your eyes,
where you need touch
and tension.

Breathe for me.

Tell me with bristles
on your skin,
where you need warmth
and soft light.

Breathe for me.

Tell me with wax
and honey,
how you want to bend
into this storm.

Breathe

and watch me
devour.

Rebellion

I think I want to steal a car and rob a bank with you. Bar fight with other men over you. Collect a few scars and point them out when I talk to other people about love. I want to cause trouble with you and not listen to what the world expects of me. Watch you bloom in the carnage of complete freedom, where the healing power of truth erupts rebellion against the weight of rules. I think I want to climb a ladder into the clouds. Each breath of ascent connected to roots of defiance scattered into the afterglow of your presence on Earth. I would look down and see you, the untamed landscape of nature being nature. The brightest lighthouse, and me, perched, hunting those looking to diminish your stellar fucking shine.

Womb

There would be no gravity without the womb.
No idea of home, or nature.
I'm not sure the ocean would move
without its million mothers
towing life to land,
currents gently swaying
between hip and heart.
Blood of love
and cruelty,
enduring the savagery
of man.
Tears and rain
and the sharpened teeth
of every feral lioness
who sprout from the same soil.
Pulp of Earth,
growing in defiance
through all the casualties,
for a touch of sunlight
and softened air.
Treetops of gold and green,
bedding for scars unseen
and ones faded
but never gone.
Up high,
becoming the stars
to guide us home,
lights living
long after death.

Communion

This communion of milk,
our feet in the dirt,
the sustenance and clay
of earth-body.
Woman king,
creator, conscious/unconscious,
everywhere, everything.
I plant immolation fields
for the bones
of brutal men
to collect in.

You

Your face, behind my eyelids,
I am asleep at the wheel,
stoned and drunk off knowing
you are out there, living, breathing,
finding new ways to see the world.
Everything, a revelation.
Let me watch you think,
fall into the tiny cracks
and turbulent beauty
of your mind on fire.
Keep me dizzy
and off-balance.
Tell me all things true,
let me not judge you
for being you.

Eyes

Vast, fathomless,
sweet crystal
of your gaze
churns a slow syrup,
treacle,
deep, rooted
to lost cosmonauts,
a basin of water
and stardust,
mixing and separating
at once,
pooling into conundrum
and comfort,
I could maybe survive the berth
if I hold my breath
and never lose focus
on the ballast point
of congruence,
where my eyes
meet yours,
an invisible knot
I trust
will never let me drown.

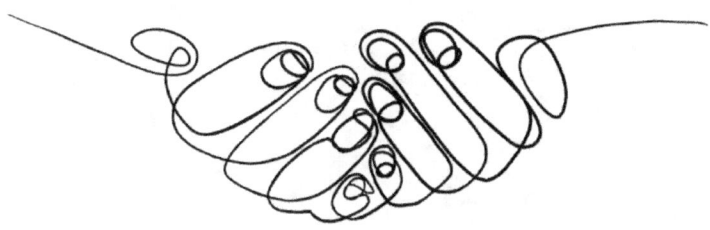

Hunger

My knees touch the floor for your mouth,
and at times, I want to command it,
tell your lips where I need them.
Write scripture about the pressure
and soft-pink fullness,
saliva more like sap
from the tree of life.
I trace lines with my finger
and hope you bite me,
draw blood,
because you are hungry
for prayer
and being bound
to muffle
and moan,
stretched round,
tight horizon
of Heaven on Earth.
Return to me with danger,
make me risk the closeness
of kissing you,
of tasting what I worship
and want to rule.

Simple

Time is paused,
and you are still,
fabric fallen,
I see more of you
and study skin
like world maps,
memorizing
shape and shadow
and the allure
of travel.
I open books and look
for better words,
more impressive ways to say it,
but simplicity
is often the greatest truth:
Beautiful,
Fascinating,
Hilarious,
Mesmerizing,
Sexy,
Interesting,
Honest,
Exact and direct
is what slips
along the air of my lungs.

Want

I want your spit and honey.
I want to taste the edge of the universe between your legs.
Slow and curious, I hold you on my tongue,
wanting nothing but a moment to feel like forever.
Count my pulse in the way you release your breath.
They are mini-deaths pledged to gods I do not know.
Ones where I invent new beliefs
based on how you're swallowed.
On how you linger in the grip of my fingers and jaw.
Show me your eyes from above.
Command me in violent stares.
Lock me into ocean sounds swirling through your thighs.
Let me chase time and the unknown.
Fold me into your flesh
and let me become part of an existence
where fear can't conquer any man
who lives inside your bones.

Ghost

I have time and thoughts,
and the night,
and you.
A ghost I can't touch,
wading in the air before my tired eyes.
A truth breaching reality,
you step through imagined doorways
and into my cells.
Haunt me,
inside out
and without remorse.
Feed the fires
that burn your name
into my bones.
Whisper into the caverns
and cold crevices
with that mouth
my mind cannot let go of.
Keep the rain for your skin
and let me be swallowed
by this welcomed pyre.
This is no tragedy.
This is the result
of man in the magic
of Mother Nature.
You are a church
of no walls
and I come carrying sins
I hope you'll approve of.

Unison

My eyes walk every fiber and flesh tone.
They linger on the places which wet my mouth.
You, a gift in the hands of a new day.
Every bow tethered to more secrets I must know.
More playful cures to my ailing heart.
I want to watch you crawl across the morning light
and consume my attention.
Beads of sweat with your name on them.
Glistening futures found along the lasting landscape of your
legs.
Life beginning where they end, in the white cotton syrup of
dripping clouds.
I want to become undone in your playhouse.
Tortured and teased by how you slink along,
your stare borrowed from the Devil.
Your body, some hypnotic serpent
asking me to return from the distractions of mankind.
Asking me to slip into something primal.
Something beyond control.
Something more like a ravenous bear waiting to be unleashed.
Ferocious and bold, and then held afterwards,
when its chest has grown warm,
two breaths dying in unison under the remaining hours of the
sun.

Bloom

I trample all other notions
to get to the place you bloom in me.
Blood and beating drums on parade,
where the synapses are as long as your legs
and the capillaries curve like your mouth.
Risking recollection of your eyes
in electric current of thought.
Lost in the danger and delicacies
of the atmosphere you spin in my head.
The bountiful ideas of how you should be touched
and taken care of.
How you should be given galaxies that match your stare.
Nebulas pulled from vulnerable depths
I cannot escape,
where the slow torture of desire chases your shadow.
These daydreams swallow hours in beautiful affliction
as you haunt me from afar.
I am a home, with an ache in its walls,
searching for your ghost
in hopes it will one day lead to your body.

Sun

If I could converse with the sun,
I'd bet it'd confess it tries to slow down for you.
I know this to be true,
because if I were it,
I'd want to hold you in the light for as long as possible.
Millions of years circling the rage of a lonely fire
in the absence of life.
Then, you, emerging from shadows,
part reflection of molten caress
and part soft silence of what visits at night.
I know it, because the saltwater reef in your eyes
and fullness of the Earth hanging off your lips
would pull me off course.
It would pull me closer to what makes a day beautiful.
Closer to what gives the faint touch of my flames purpose.
Closer to you.

Dream

When I'm alone,
and the world is dead,
I find you in the moonlight
against my window.
I see futures, impossible.
Where pretty things
and ocean's end
are hopeful ideas
kept behind the quiet night
of my lips.

There is no artificial light here.
Not with the way you glow,
buzzing in waves,
matter in motion,
even in still frame.

I want to build a little home for my mouth in your neck.
I want to undress our fears with love.
I want to do more than dream.

Pussy

There is light and life in this waking dream.
Heaven's gate seems to exist
for a heathen like me.
And I pine for new religion.
For bliss in the balm of madness.
Tucked into my mind,
portraits of you,
their colors wet with oxygen.
Flesh of fruit becomes all memory.
The cup of eternity overflows.
The power and truth
of new beginnings.
Sweet sap for forgotten veins.
Every seed and star
and happy death of man
salivating for your medicine.

Mantis

It eats my head now
It devours my soft soul
The mantis loves me

www.ingramcontent.com/pod-product-compliance
Lightning Source LLC
Chambersburg PA
CBHW070454130626
46553CB00006B/2407